VIA Folios 185

One Trail of Longing,
Another of String

Published by Bordighera Press, an imprint of the John D. Calandra Italian American Institute of Queens College, The City University of New York.

25 West 43rd Street, 17th Floor, New York, NY 10036

Library of Congress Control Number: 2025942478

Cover image by Jr Korpa from Upsplash.

VIA Folios 185
ISBN 978-1-59954-240-9

ONE TRAIL OF LONGING, ANOTHER OF STRING

Carla Panciera

B

BORDIGHERA PRESS

For Rebecca, of course

Table of Contents

IV.

and that // was the last time, for a long time, that she spoke about the past.

MARIE HOWE
"Marie (Reprise)"

I

Like Enough, Like Belonging

My daughter calls me to see five birds
at the feeder this morning. *Yes,* I say.
I think I say. *I see.* Eye rings.
Wing bars. Crown stripes. I did not
give birth to all my daughters. No matter
if I have sought, not sought, complexity,
it has found me. It does matter
where one comes from. That miracle,
those old questions. House or purple finch.
Song or chipping sparrow. What help
can I offer any living creatures?
Those borne of me, those entrusted
to my care? The winters here are hard.
Yet birds flutter and light despite
arctic gusts. Chickadees become experts
in shivering. We wonder where they rest,
why they stay, how they will survive,
if a season exists which feels to them
like enough, like belonging.

This Nothing Like Forgiveness

The red-tail is a regular in the hayfield. We share the kind of silence said to build brain cells in mice.

I missed the fall migration. *Nothing to see now*, someone said, *unless you want to see raptors*. He shuddered as if I'd suggested vivisection, body snatching, a cataloging of parasites.

I'm trying to learn something, I wanted to say. But it embarrassed me, the need to know red-tail, from Cooper's, from sharp-shinned. How to reconcile what we want with what makes sense to want.

I have caused others' pain. I'm sorry, though I've never said so. And now, this love of birds, these creatures indifferent and alert. This nothing that will redeem me.

I confess: It matters that the hawk stays even though it is there to break the necks of other creatures I love: the finches that spiral up from the alfalfa, the young rabbits.

This is the damnable indulgence, the way we can't be free of this world. The hawk stays, at least for now, so I stay, too, until crows reclaim the field, sociable amidst the stubble.

In the Movie of My Dreams of You

Dock bones warming
        our shoulders

                    spiderleg tapping board slats—sun? sun?

you say, don't be afraid, though something pricks
        vertebrae   here?   here?

you say   I'll be here

there's no one else   just you, the limit of my limbic my

              every repression
and its subsequent explosion

                        my metaphor

you waltz into my dream, tap shoes and a Solo cup,

        a store-bought Danish,   a flea-addled dog
the dog looks like Johnny Depp and then

        he is and I'm wishing I had worn something
besides my bathing suit

and you?   you are
              playing with his hair

        you who
are the pocket of my most comfortable jeans

into which I stash my Kleenex and
        my indiscretions, murmuring   our horoscopes

                                  Is anyone watching this?

What did you expect? that same river beside which
        we sunned ourselves?
                        Remember

these are just   pictures—
        cinematic flashes of amygdala

        (how   they   lure)
Remember   you

said yes here   here is where I'll be
from now on

        this is not prognostication

these are not oracles   bloody lipped, offering hymns
this is just when sleep is most like wakefulness

        your shoulders are sunburned and this is still
        when that was a good thing

you are   saying: isn't the water beautiful?

                      something's tickling

the small of my back   fingertip? fingertip?

        you

show me the veins on the underside
        of your wrist and I think:

if I touch them I will feel a current

you are my message from the gods

                           when I wake
                           the sun on my chest is archetype
                  reminder

we can never start here again
      where you are

close enough to hear me
      call   you

      to say don't be afraid

of pictures.

Reliquary, Shadowbox

Lamplighters whistled their approach and no wonder.
Shadows form now. Vision blurs.
The early dark, a flock of turkeys along my walking route.
How many waxing moons like this exist in poems?
Longing rises for trimmed wicks, flames to star the way ahead.
I imagine pinsetters' fathers at home drinking whiskey
because my uncle set pins and that's what his father would do.
Lamplighters collected miller moths, beetles in a glass, stymied
    pickpockets and thieves.
Ice cutters lost horses in the river. But not in November.
Is it too late now to wonder if anything I've done has been enough?
My poor uncle describes the rabbits running through his room all night.
Some mornings ice forms on granite's imperfections.
Still, I have no urge to be inside when outside is slick with collagists'
    leaves.
I envy the turkeys, stoic and on guard. They can't be startled or nostalgic.
They are not subject to. Not so the rest of us. The penitent,
the bobbin boy, the wet nurse, the supplier of leeches.

Why I Don't Keep a Diary

7 am. No moon, but yesterday, a supermoon in a splotchy sky. A pink and blue sunrise so sweet, it was embarrassing to point out. You wouldn't want the photograph of it on a calendar.

8:56 am: Lines at gas pumps before the bomb cyclone arrives. If it's true that the Inuit have 100 words for snow, are any of them bomb cyclone?

Ten days since I last touched my mother's hair. Since that one thing still felt like her.

11:47 am: My students shares fears. *What about you, Jason?* He says: *The quadruple 'S': Snakes, spiders, sharks, scorpions.* Pauses. *Oh. And love.*

4:23 pm: sunset. Yesterday: 4:22. Every day: sunset.

What if I keep my mother's watch close to me because I think it might still be warm from her wrist, but I don't touch it so I can never find out? What if seas rise beneath brilliant sunsets, clouds flamelike above the roiling? What if I am not sorry that I see some beauty in that?

6:32 pm: For supper, I make a pizza and cry. Because I can't remember if you're supposed to use olive oil or shortening on the pan before you roll out the dough.

Because I thought I could just call my mother and ask. Even when I knew, when it had been made clear to me via grim red dye and physicians, that her death was imminent. Even then, I never considered writing down the answer.

10:02 pm: Into the dark, I say, *Hurricane. Cyclogenesis. Bombogenesis.* They summon neither wind nor sleep. I consider years when I hung calendars where I would see them first thing in the morning. How dutifully I flipped the page when the old month ended, how faithfully I admired the new.

If there are a hundred words for love then what about its lingering?

Phantom

*Plum Island, a wild and fantastical sand beach, is thrown
up by the joint power of winds and waves into the thousand
wanton figures of a snow drift.* Joshua Coffin, 1845

Black-backed gulls view panoramas
     of a place

            where beach plums once crowned dunes, part river's
bottom,
part sea's.

Here, time
   elapses tide by tide, the Atlantic

part Arctic, part appetite. This is what's left: Ice Age
water, winds that curl,
            ghost dunes that crest into waves atop which teeter

dining rooms, a chaise lounge.

So you thought you could stay?

     A barrier island's function is change;
         the sea—the current's yeoman, the implacable sculptor—
ferries sand north to south.

Twelve thousand years, you think, is tide enough for art.

     But the moon—part silver, part
        master—summons its shore and   leaves

the sand pockmarked by filter feeders,

sets the gulls aloft.

In this world, part wind, part waves, the fanciful
            is hope, phantom-like
the insistence
of your own ornamentations..

Smart Girls Always Have a Plan

If only my teachers had told me:
Math is movement trying to express itself.

If they had shown me the Incan *quipu*—
llama hair fanned out like a sun in kinesthetic base tens?

I'm listening. *Math*, after all, is one letter removed
from stories of the gods.

But those algorithmic days, I coveted cloud paths,
the thoughtless sweep of a janitor's broom.

If someone had mentioned Galileo
who believed the universe could only be read in shapes—

who said: we wander a dark labyrinth without these—
Reading, I understood. Labyrinths.

Which brings me to Ariadne. Didn't everyone assume
it was impossible to get out of that thing alive?

Even the hero's faithless father prepared himself
for a namesake sea.

But Ariadne was like those high school calculus queens.
So many of us saw chicken scratch, a traitorous alphabet.

But those girls intuited north. And maybe, after all
her figuring, Ariadne was abandoned by her love.

Or maybe the other version is true:
that grief itself left the fatal sails unfurled.

This is why, of course, some people prefer mathematics.
They desire unicursal endings.

I prefer a world both art and science, full of possibilities
I might discover, one trail of longing, another of string.

Someone Asks Me To Consider Time

Kant says time is neither event nor thing.

Well, I think. That's that.

Sundials, T-squares,
heartbeats, the equinox.
In places of worship, incense burns.
All to mark no thing.

But Teresa calls.
She's found my letters.
There are dead dogs in them, old boyfriends;
the miscarriage is happening,
(has happened)
and I have to catch a plane.
The plane has   (not yet)
taken off.

Here, wind moves water in one direction,
then another. Some mornings
nothing ripples, not leaves,
not iridescence on birdwing, beetle back.
Some mornings
both: stillness, unrest.

Last season's loon calls.
And sometimes? I can't remember the lake
where I first heard that sound,
though the vision of it rises
through a paint-flecked pane.

On my morning walk, a hawk
perched on a telephone wire
above what used to be a hayfield:
rusted New Holland baler,
bobolinks and meadowlarks
saved from the mower
a generation ago,
dead farmers, dead cows.

Now
is not the time,
moles, voles, mice,
to dart into the light
though nothing stops in stillness
except solstice
when the sun stands still in declination.

I should tell someone this,
that we are not propelled beyond a moment
of observation, even loss, into something else:
field edge, lakeside, motherhood.
Instead, we are always
on our way.

On my return, the wire's empty.
The hawk has hunted or not,
is sated
or continues,
hungry.
Hunger, at least, returns.

Once, in different water,
my daughters waded naked
after mussels. Appendages,
these daughters were. I was
accustomed to the creases
behind their knees
where I kept their pulse.

Now, on a floating dock,
my daughters sun themselves, swing limbs
above water that soon enough
will be ice.

Ships' bells and steeple chimes,
an hourglass,
the pharaoh's water clock.

These days, you can lift saliva
off the back of a stamp,
determine who licked it.
And that woman?
That sender?

She will have stopped
and she will
not yet
have stopped   and she will still be

bleeding.

II

The Requirements of an Injured Hawk

Make sure it is grounded, not guarding a kill. Go home for gloves.
Leave the dog. Avoid the beak, the talons. No babytalk. No crying.

Tuck the wings. Do not try to make it drink. Do not spoon-feed.

Cover the head. The hawk will close one eye and dream
panoramically. Ledge-height, cliffside, full-color views of the world
that would make you dizzy. Everything below triangulated, oblivious.

Do not sing. Especially do not sing.

It will be your first car ride with a hawk in a box beside you. You will
imagine it springing up from its shock, its sudden wingspan wide as
the fields you pass. Feathers at your earlobe, talons at your neck.

Instead, there will be silence and you will consider lullabies to fill it.
You will imagine what it listens for. But it isn't song. It's owls.

You will have no idea what the bird makes of its pain. No idea of
maggots already at the wound.

Keep driving. Remind yourself: This hawk, too, is motherless.

Sunday Nights the Widows Came to Dinner

After my father left for milking, the women
lit cigarettes while I cleared the table,
ran hot water that steamed the window.
Smoke curled from my mother's mouth.
Don't tell your father, she said.
What did they talk about while I worried
that my homework wasn't done?
I long to sit with them again, these women
finished with part of their lives, women as mesmerizing
as the sparks from the welding torch
my father used to repair a hitch. *Don't look*,
he would caution. *This will blind you.*

When the women left, I went outside
to clean the ashtrays, my mother beside me
to watch cars pull away. *This is when
I feel the worst for them*, she'd say.
In my memory it is always November.
So much of the cold ahead, and dark, and darker
still once they had gone and my mother
went inside to the television. *Stay*, I would say,
if I could talk to her now. *Stay here where
everything still belongs to us: the yellow light
and fields of stubble, autumn's smoke.*

After My Mother Requests a Parent-Teacher Conference

Fifty years after we have missed our library time,
       and Miss Johnston pounds her desk and says,

Goddamnit, and we stare at our hands desperate
       for the bell to ring so the starlings of our laughter

can burst forth, scooping the wet air of April,
       and fifty years after Miss Johnston says, *If*

some parent wasn't trying to run this school thinking
       she knows everything, a person could think,

fifty years after my classmates turn to me,
       the girl whose mother has brought this fury down

upon us, I can still imagine my mother at home
       ironing the spring curtains or serving her old nurse friend

leftover shepherd's pie then giving her a perm,
       and I know Miss Johnston doesn't think I should read

as much as I do, and my mother, who reads romance
       novels and *True Confessions Magazine*, who sends me

in each month with my Scholastic book order (perfect change
       from the money my father keeps on the barn windowsill

from when the old Italians come for raw milk to make cheese)
       wants to know why reading is discouraged in Miss Johnston's class,

fifty years and still shame prickles its fireflies around me,
        embers disturbed by a draft that comes out of the dark

with some beauty in it and some pain and the ability to burn
        holes in the shirt my mother found at the Fall River outlets

and that I had chosen so thoughtlessly, I wished my mother
        had been as invisible as any other mother, a mother who didn't

think there was only one world, I want to say, not to my mother
        or to Miss Edith Johnston, but to those children in that
        terrible room:

We will fill in the dots with no stray marks on our Iowa tests,
        and open our mouths for the soggy carton's rim, for milk
        that tastes

nothing like the milk my mother pours when I get home,
        and smell ourselves for the first time the way others smell us,

but we won't be here forever and there is so much time
        for someone to love you the way my mother loves.

Wishful

What if we could have known each other as girls?
You could have milked a cow by hand, my father pausing
the way he never paused, to show you how.

The calves would have sucked your fingers and you might
have liked it, surprised by their rough tongues,
by the way they'd keep calling you back.

On a granite wheel in the garage,
my father would have sharpened our sled blades,
and we would drag them to the far pasture's hill.

You would have been afraid to walk past the cows,
and I would have pretended to be braver than I felt
because I would have wanted nothing to scare you away.

I would have told you that the hill ended
in the cows' burial grounds. Bones under snow.
In the spring, you might return to see them.

We would dry our mittens on silver radiators,
my mother already in her blue chenille bathrobe
heading to bed with Vicks 44 and a romance novel.

You might have noticed: my house always smelled
a little of cows. In the morning, the sound of my father
stirring his coffee too long would wake you.

On the counter, the dough would be rising, my mother
setting out the powdered sugar and jam. Sometimes,
she served pie for breakfast, too.

Out the window, the cows would file up
to be milked, their breath, their enormous bodies,
steaming up the walkway to the barn.

I would have been sorry to be left alone with my parents.
Lonesome, was a word my father used,
my mother and I at the window watching you go.

Offertorium

Mom, I said once. *My sneaker's full of blood.*
In those days, there was always blood:

mice she trapped in cupboards, the bluefish her brothers
caught at the lighthouse and brought her to gut.

One Christmas she gave me a spoon ring, a red Panasonic Dynamite 8 track.
Northern Isle sweaters with matching dickies.

No one ever knew what to buy her.
Later, we threw out Yankee Candles, souvenir potholders.

She always knew a priest for holy water and palms. *I miss the Mass in Latin,*
she told me. This struck me because she let everything else go.

What I loved: finding her the first figs of the season
and how she ate them all at once and made herself sick.

I have a scar on my ankle. From something she told me not to do.
I have her wedding ring, the same veins in my hands.

Nights that last year, I blessed her with the holy water, a joke we shared.
I went to Mass with my sisters when I was five because they promised
    donuts.

They knew, didn't they? My sisters. What she did when we left the house.
A hundred acres and our mother, locked in the bathroom with a pack
    of Winstons.

Her hair, her breath, the shoulder of her sweater, all
the holes and the spaces and the blood of her reeking.

But I came home anyway to breathe next to her.
I closed the bathroom window, kept the smoke in.

Heirloom

In the picture window of the house she lived in
with her new husband, my sister put a lamp on a table,
an antique oil lamp, rewired, beneath a painted globe.

When we drove by, my mother noticed if the light
was on, if the drapes were opened, closed.
I had gotten my license and she insisted I practice.

Find mountains in the seascape. Black ice. Startled antlers.
Develop a sense of north, she said. *Keep money in the glovebox,
in the heel of your shoe.* Pretend what rattles is windshear.

My sister marked every event by the dress she wore to it.
My mother by how many pounds of potato salad she made,
how many meatballs. Me by words that no one said.

Or by what was told to me alone to keep to myself.
All I ever wanted to be was a housewife like your sister,
my mother said, a few months before she died.

She did not add: And a waitress, a farm wife.
My sister and my mother hung curtains depending on the season,
exchanged the language of valances and panels.

Eventually, leaving a lover's bed, I watched sunrises
on the Turnpike, drove stick, top down on the convertible
all winter, flawed sense of direction.

I should have died a hundred times.
How helpful could I have been to them,
those women whose days began with letting in the light?

Her Again

Corinne's sister wants to make a scrapbook for her birthday.
We turn 59 this year. No milestone except

we're fifteen years older than their mother would ever be.
I've wondered during the silence between us

these four decades, if Corinne inherited some lethal strand,
and would someone think to let me know if—

Why would anyone in that family remember
my name? Especially this sister, with whom I've never

exchanged a word. These sisters with perfect smiles
generations before routine orthodonture.

Now one writes: *When our father sold
the house he threw everything out.*

My own house was burned to the ground.
This, she would not know. Or

that I stood over its foundation, small as a root cellar, crawling
with brambles. Easy to imagine

you made the whole thing up. Speaking of the unimaginable:
She wants images of Corinne

at the fair with a calf. That one aberrant season of strange
expertise. My place in the universe in exchange

for her mother's empty rooms. I could write: *Emmy, your sister*
had enough of me. For what offense, I can't recall. I do

remember being banned from her lunch table.
The high school cafeteria has no doubt withstood

all carnage and remains as innocuous as the bin
into which I've packed a few things away.

I can waste all day stewing. Revel in it. Instead, I go
to the attic and say aloud, *I'm part of nothing now.*

But there she is. I had forgotten the cakes we made
when we were bored. Box cakes. Store-bought frosting.

Air-hockey game on the table, centerpiece shoved aside.
Had forgotten that seam in the linoleum.

It caught our socks as we slid into the room
to my mother's summons.

The light in the attic defies attics. Sun. Sun. Sun.
I sit in it and study the way things were built—

Hand-hewn. Home-forged. Mortise and tenon.
Corinne's image in my lap. I bought a yoked sweater like that.

Tried to ski because she loved it, learned to fold notes
the way she did. *Emmy, I tried everything.*

Now, I expect to feel something. Longing. Pain. Relief.
At the very least, hours away from and years older than I was

then. Everything that has played out as the sun stretches
a rhombus of light through this space, is as ineffable, as

inconceivably impermanent as the granite doorstep I trod
each afternoon, opening our back door after leaving your sister

staring into her locker, calculating, with admirable focus,
what to take along with her, what could be left behind.

The Mere Pleasure of God

Mid-June, our pastures reduced
to dandelion, thistle, Donna and I
sit on a rock, pass a joint that someone
left in the ashtray of Donna's car.
Soon, the cows, done milking,
will tramp out to investigate.

There's a boy who's taken me
to the slippery places. A carnal boy,
some rum cokes and a stick shift.
School's out. This dominion
is cowpies, black flies. A lack
of algebra. The sun incensed.

I don't need the cattle's fiery stares,
flared nostrils streaming snot,
bunch of disciples with a pipeline
to my father. But hither they come,
hurrying as soon as they spot us,
empty bags swinging like church purses.

Midwife in the Cowbarn

Farmer calls me for a bug-eyed heifer,
so far gone she's liable to bleed to death or bolt.

Lie down. Lie down, he says.
But, tied so tight, she won't.

He slaps her flank and hollers. She blows snot,
and, new at this, yanks hard against the rope.

I ask him if he sings. Then: *Nevermind*,
approach her slow to pull the slipknot free.

When her head drops, I catch her wild eye,
speak the low notes of the confessor.

Soon as she listens, I run my hand along her spine
shoulder to tailhead. Cow holds her breath, considers.

When I reach inside her, shoulder-deep
and cheek to pin bone, she's steady as an old girl.

Legs splayed, small udder stretched,
she pants, then waits, inflates her barrel.

Basso profundo. Yes. She knows those words,
bows her back and summons muscle.

Inside, my fingers find a leg cocked as if to prance.
Sometimes that's all it is—stubborn knuckle.

The pearl white hoof is an arrow to air. Then: the pair.
The rest she'll do her scared-stiff self.

Her baby's nostrils twitch; his eyes emerge and blink.
First time, the ears flick forward.

Calf, there is a drop from here, slick-shouldered
dive into a place with few alternatives.

Last push is fluid-filled calf-sprawl in rising steam.
His dam, surprised to see him there, commences licking.

He sits up, shakes fluid out his ears.
Warm milk jets from swollen teats.

The farmer is a boy, big-handed.
I see that now. Stubborn fields. Winters ahead.

Tomorrow, he'll put the calf on a truck veal-bound.

The dam, high strung, will send the machine flying.
Outside, she'll bellow, pace the barnyard gate.

Winter Baby

Tell me the truth, I said to my friend,
who had just given birth. *How bad is it?*
You won't believe the blood, she said,
for which truth, I am indebted,

and January, especially, is no time
for something so bloody, so lousy
with fluid. But there you were staring up
at me, wondering, what happens next?

Nights, as you nursed (I never refused you),
I read a novel where one character
is castrated, one loses his legs to infection,
another throws himself in front of a train.

A different friend, also a mother,
recommended this book. Said I would love it.
My god. I thought my most obvious flaw
was a too prominent nose.

While your father slept in another room,
the wind kept me awake after you fell back to sleep.
You and I alone in the kind of winter
in which deer starve.

People will tell you, baby, this month is named
for a god who can look both forward and back.
Other babies will embrace that. Don't you.
What good did the old gods ever offer?

What use would they be in this formidable dark?
In January, it is impossible to imagine
the color of grass, though we form a belief
in dull-knifed amputations.

We embrace the kind of despair that convinces us
everyone, everyone
is speeding away somewhere else
and only violence might stop them.

I bled for months after you were born
and couldn't get anyone to believe me.
I thought it mattered, their acknowledgement.
Then I realized: No one knows me.

But, listen, baby, the days are already lengthening.
January comes from the Latin word
for door. Remember that.
How it is in its nature to open.

III

The Orchid Hour

Pink outer whorls,
resupinate lips,
these sexy birds
have nothing to do but wait.

We are wired for it:
their finicky bait,
their inflorescence
set loose on windowsills.

Their symmetry is a twist
that will upend us,
their lippy breath elixir,
patient as a trap.

As if Faith Has Anything To Do With It

Not exactly a room of one's own,
            this soccer mom chair by the river,

boys making bacon on the open fire
            behind me, girls trying to drink

strong coffee black. Chipmunk.
            Deer flies. A morning-after

bottle rocket and the predictable
            barking response. And, okay,

the light on the river, birdsong,
            blah, blah, blah—everything

that's ever been in a poem plus
            bacon, and who can write, anyway,

with twelve boys trapped in a cave
            two miles underwater, and when,

last night, in a darkness so blinding,
            I had to wave and wave my

hand in front of my face and it
            didn't guarantee *next*, didn't allow

me to fall asleep and believe in
            something as mundane as morning.

But here it is, and birds *do* sing,
      much earlier than we think they do,

drowning out crickets and the yearning
      we have for both knowing and not

knowing what will happen next,
      what weight snapped sticks last night

in the underbrush just outside our skin.
      Other people provide miracles,

bring boys back to the light, and birds
      sing because, one theory suggests,

they have survived the night, sing
      with the kind of cock-a-hoop resolve

I want to lift with tongs from the fire,
      my mouth watering in anticipation.

In the Car She Drives, the Air Is Always Fresh(ened)

A cardboard pine tree of Caribbean Colada swings from the rearview mirror, the mirror in which my daughter considers whether she needs eyelash extensions, teeth whitening. Whether she needs her eyebrows threaded. Onto the vents, she's clipped mini-clothespins of Catching Rays. Somewhere, Fresh Cotton has lodged itself to participate in the olfactory assault.

When I come home and ask why the car has to smell like a corny souvenir shop, she says, disgusted: *Corny? What does that even mean?* I stumble towards the medicine cabinet for anything to ward off the migraine the combined toxins stoke over my left eyebrow (which does need threading but which, to my daughter's horror, I pluck—pluck!—as if I have just finished following behind the mules breaking sod in Nebraska Territory).

Okay, I manage. *Like a perfume factory. Like a Glade collision on the interstate. Like the senior center ladies lunch. Like some coked-up, hybrid-assed funeral arrangement from hell.*

I think we are about to have it now, the you-don't-get-me-cuz-if-you-did-you-would-see-what-part-of-our-family's-fucked-up-ness-I-am-trying-to-mask blow out. Instead, she turns from where she is rummaging through a drawer full of aux cords, earbuds, keys, and says, *Hybrid-assed?*

Then she is laughing—at me, not with me. But I know we will be fine because my polluted head hurts so bad that when I try to focus on her, I see not one, but two of her beautiful selves searching.

Feast

When she is starving herself.

When she lets her bones rise like the wreck of the Frances
at the convergence of minus tides, new moons,
after a winter of super storms:

When you consider the thumb-sucking lap-sitter
she was—that angle only she will ever have of your face
from the underside of your jaw:

When you can't think why she takes the meat
off this beautiful body, this body whose thighs
whose elbows   earlobes—

               the soap-bubble-limbed, mosquito-scabbed
                 flesh of this sea monster baby:

When she talks the way she's always talked
a teaspoonful-by-teaspoonful elocution
       and she worries about missing algebra—

When you think: All this? All this and not
the necessary thing?

When you wonder how you did this to her,
and when she turns a song up so you can hear:

Think of the ways we wash ashore.

In Truro, for example, a shipwreck place
where Pamet Indians smoked tobacco in lobster claw pipes,
and Pilgrims, seasick, filthy, finally touched land.

This place of purse nets and mute swans, a world
where gods had to be appeased, not stationed
in a bed of peonies and painted every summer

        like the virgins of our childhood.
        This place to raise a glass against sacrifice.

(You can't help that she's in you still, can't imagine
the way she began, the spiraling vessels,
the blinking heart—that terrible miracle, that return guest.)

        Yes. Let's set the table in Truro one day.
        White-candle drip castles indelible on cloth.

When your rib cage plays back the ghost of her alto—

Let's find the first tomatoes of the season, a fingerbowl of sea salt.
Let us, if this is what the world asks of us, beg forgiveness.
But then let's eat. Let's use our hands.

For Homework I Told Sixteen Girls To Break Some Rules

I should have seen it coming when they brewed tea in class on Fridays. When they plugged too many kettles in at once. Scorned the use of sugar. Ignored the warning bell. They stayed in the library after hours. Pilfered string beans from the salad bar at Whole Foods. Walked one kilometer of a 5K and wore the t-shirt anyway. The substitute teacher could not stop them from dancing. When poems moved them, they cheered. Cried. Left the room without asking. Later, they mocked archetypes, especially those representing spring. One weekend, thirsty, adrift, they helped themselves to lemonade and cookies in the lobby of Salem's Hawthorne Hotel. That winter, they hennaed each other with invisible ink, materialized first in line for grand openings, for concerts on school nights. By choice, they became bad listeners. *We can't possibly be expected to raise our hands.* One teacher sent an anonymous email comparing them to a man who snuck into Yellowstone and was killed by a hot spring. Anonymous except the girls knew who sent it, memorized his address, nursed a shared resentment for metaphors not of their making.

Our Boldest Child: A Chronicle

She marched ahead of us down every trail, sometimes naked. Hands behind her back, she nosed snakes and hornets. How we dreaded playground climbing structures, parking lots, the stepladders stock boys left in the Home Depot aisle.

We were unprepared for her, couldn't anticipate impulse: tasting battery acid, for example, or the pink plastic egg that fit so perfectly in her throat. Not a climb up a ladder, but a climb up the slide. One bone broken and set without morphine.

Such relief when she didn't like the water. Swim bubble strapped to her back, she stayed dry. Poolside, we read. We had almost forgotten reading. Yes, we thought, this is what it feels like to look away.

And that day, before the splash, we heard the slap of feet on concrete, the silence of her, mid-air. We sprang up out of our own shoes as she exploded to the surface, spouting water, like an oracle who foretold: There is nothing left but fear.

On Days Like This

Outside, well fed jays in brilliant plumage,
though plumage is a peacock word, a bird who
plumes. The temperature, minute by minute,
plummets. A plume of chimney smoke, and words
that bridge dark water days. Waterways. Blue
jays. My mother's way of clearing her throat. Blue-
throated birds, hoarse with squawking. Throaty
voices, sooty voices, tar in the lungs. Hidden
packs of Winstons. Once the cold sets in, so many
questions. The waves spume white. Ice water
hurts lungs. The longing for my mother bridges
ribs. Weather like this sticks in my throat. Off
plumb means out of true. Today, the ocean will be
cold (the lungs, the longing, too) and blue.

When We Come Without Our Daughters and Still Leave Them Behind

When we leave the campground we won't interrupt
their trek through the nature path identifying Indian paintbrush,
their single-file determination, their bent heads.

Or their search for marshmallow sticks in the pines
beside our site. They won't be coming any moment
into the clearing to unfold their chairs around the fire.

One won't appear cupping a red newt in her palm,
another a shredded elbow, their hair unbrushed for days,
their pierced ears newly healed.

On the picnic table, a centerpiece of moth wing, snake
skin. But there will be no way to meet them, no way
to gather up those girls who reek of bug spray and smoke.

Instead, we'll leave them here ignoring us as we drive by
the river, where they won't still wait, nets poised, for crayfish
with the nature center guide, their summer crush.

We'll want to stop, of course, to ask what they have found,
fearing one or another's heartache, but we will think
we have no time to stop, or plenty.

We will have left one water shoe behind.

All the Summers

I tell my daughters about the morning my mother
saw a heifer in the cornfield, went outside
in her bathrobe and said, *Kandi, is that you?*

Kandi strolled to the back steps like another aunt
arriving for coffee.

My mother had no halter,
could not have used it if she had.

*But Kandi didn't need a rope! She'd follow you anywhere!
She came when you called her name!*

My girls nod. *Fascinating stuff,* they're thinking.
Pass the cream cheese.

My mother didn't believe a cow would do that, either.
I could not convince her.

Until Kandi followed her to my bedroom window
where the cow's wet muzzle
left rainbow prisms on my screen.

The idiosyncrasies of animals and loved ones
must (mustn't they?) swirl around us still?

I might ask my girls this as they scroll.

When she grew up, all black except for the white rind
of her belly, Kandi could unlatch the milkhouse door with her tongue.

The other cows—cows-in-waiting, sorority sister cows,
precursors to book groups and knit-night gatherings
of females wine-drunk and appetizered out—followed her.

Her herd was full of grand champions, big, white, Marilyn-esque
beauties, famous for their pink udders and eyelashes.

Kandi had folklore. She had wit.
The route she foresaw to the feeders full of grain!

One daughter rises to clear plates, rests a hand
on my shoulder.

Her sisters slip arms into coat sleeves.

So! So! I scrubbed her belly.
You will be the first in your bloodline to go to college, I told her.

You could joke like that with Kandi.

My daughters don't believe in cows like that
anymore than their grandmother did.

Faith shouldn't require evidence you can tie a rope around,
evidence whose heart you can feel beating in its brisket.

They don't even ask what happened to Kandi,
and I'm relieved, because I don't know.

My father bought a padlock. I left for college.

But you're the keepers of this, I say, standing in my empty kitchen.

Who else will remember how my mother allowed me
to insist on the ridiculous?

And what to do with it now? That summer of Kandi's brilliance?
All the summers?

If you believe there was a Kandi. If you're listening.

IV

From the Hollow Ends of Pipe, Yellow Jackets
Stung Our Lips When We Tried to Trumpet

The cousin
       most likely to pronounce
the summer dares
       warned:
The swingset
       will tip over if you
keep going
       so high.

Posts thudded   heartsounds,
       drumbeats,
ululation. I
       want to say   I
kept going
       anyway,
the rhythm my pulse
       now, systolic, systolic,   say
that I'd seen
       barn swallows and this
felt blue
       as wings as
silver underbellies   shocking
       my hair metallic
magnetic
                air.

I pumped.

                My skirt
lifted, lifted, fell.
                It let the sky in   I thought
if I jumped now now
                could I
fly.
                One cloud, two
the swallow babies
                perched roof-edge
the darting mother—
                followmefollowme—
the tilting world
                I carved   a smile
my mouth hurt
                from laughing   I
kicked off
                my shoes   my shoes
flew
                like fledglings
graceless, aloft
                an impossible
                                        lurch

but
my cousin understood
gravity

wouldn't listen   (who would?)
                when anyone tried
                to explain
the earthly proofs   of joy.
She knew the world
I dreamt
could right itself.

        I toed the earth
toed it until
dust
was the only thing

rising.

The Riparian Dreams of Hawks

Stream beds. Leaf hustle in the understory. The carcass of dove
meat in the cache, plucked clean of feathers.

The husbandry that refills sunflower seeds, millet, lures ground
feeders. The topiary from which songbirds might be sprung upon at
thistle.

Wishbones split in pursuit of prey. The male Cooper's' flesh
offerings and obeisance. Their mistletoe love nests. Their
cannibalistic mates.

Even my mother, fluting pie crust, spooning sugar, knitting booties,
dreamt knife blades sharp as talons.

What There Was to Fall From

Kitten head on the back steps.
Where the calf's horn
burned off incomplete,
a whipmark of red
glistens. Maggots ooze.
When you drag a dead cow out
to the burial grounds? Gravel
rubs meat off her hip bone, off
one side of her skull. If a steer
lies down on a pitchfork
you put your foot against his belly,
reclaim the tines. Snakes
in the haymow. Rats in the barn.
You dream, sometimes, the house
is haunted. This is years later,
and other people you know?
They dream the same.
What was there to fall from?
When did it begin?
The stillborn fetus
slick with membrane,
the tumorous dog.
One time? Some crazy boy
set the woods on fire.
Sometimes you ask for something
you can't have. Sometimes
you see it anyway.
How it could have been
bloodless, how you might
have remembered
the start.

Parable

The calf wandered down the driveway
and Louie, thinking: *deer*, got his gun.
But when the little Jersey emerged
from the buzzing haze of spring,
Louie lay the gun across his lap,
called: *Here, Calfie, Calfie*,
and the calf, Liza-lashed, a starlet
on mother-of-pearl hooves, came.

Louie had no rope, but you can't sit forever,
your arm around a calf's neck, even one
as satiny (oh, love! to smell like
sun and milk!) as this one.
Finally, with an extension cord leash,
they set off to find the owner.

The end of the story goes something
like this: Louie buys the calf. Feeds it
grain sweet as brown sugar, hay
festooned with alfalfa's purple blooms.
One January, he stuns it, slits
its throat, the black eyes filmy, exiting.

The beginning, naturally, remains unaltered:
The unpaved road landmarked
with potholes, the provocation of (finally!)
spring. That day, the wind crooned—
treetopstreetopstreetops, while a man
led a calf with an extension cord.

They looked, for all the world
(a stonewall of chipmunks, a forest floor
of hermit thrush and mushrooms,
a mayfly constellation) as if
in search of an outlet, some arboreal current
to prove: these things, too, exist.

To the Specialist

You take the same exit, my sister said,
that we used to take for the fair.

We have few landmarks from our new lives.
Instead, we know the strip mall
where the man lived who made rope halters;
the town where we brought plow blades
to be sharpened; the street in Johnston
where we took calves to be butchered.

Where we baled hay: housing development.
Where we grazed heifers: golf course, parking lot.

The old memories might make me pause—
show day cattle sudsy with Wisk at the wash racks,
bloodied snake pieces in the still-warm bale,
the library-like shelves of tractor parts behind men
who smelled of rubber and diesel,
new rope's splinters in palm flesh, fingers—

Except there's a new thing to consider: The doctor
says something about sugar triggering the dye.

The red areas on the scan show activity.
Activity in my family, until now,
was the most meritable thing. Also a strong back,
the ability to drive standard, a lack of squeamishness.
I don't look away. The lungs. One rib. The spine.
Belatedly, I remember to hold my mother's hand.

The spine, the doctor says, (a bad dresser in a polyester suit,
clogs). *The spine is what worries me most.*

Well, my mother says. (A wet day. Another one.
She insists we eat. So we are in the car
trying to find a breakfast place
on the same road as the Baileys' farm.
The Baileys' farm, at least, still exists.)
Everyone dies of something.

They have thick hair, calves, curls
over their polls that you can lock your fingers in.

At the butcher's in Johnston, we would wake the calf,
hand its halter to someone who told us: *Wait here,*
then head back to the heated cab, turn the radio up.
Before the song ended, the butcher returned
with the halter, a brown bag of tongue and liver
that warmed our laps on the ride home.

Artifact: September, 1963

My mother holds me on her hip in a cornfield. Though I can't see her feet, she must be standing on stubble, or between the rows of stubble where the earth will be dry. She looks away from the camera. This is the moment when she will try to get me to see my father. My mother's voice against my face. My father who will be driving the one row chopper felling corn, his seat far above the truck that follows beside him. He will look down to make sure whoever is driving the truck stays level with him so that the corn falls into the bed. My mother is not pointing. At the end of each day, when my father finished milking, he lay down beside me on the living room rug and we listened to Benny Goodman records. I kicked my feet. He called this dancing. *So long as you have her*, my mother would have said, *I'm going to bed.* But we might not have paid attention. Nights when I woke, my father got up to give me my bottle. Heating it was the only time he turned on the stove. But in this picture, daylight. My mother in long shorts with piping down the front, a sleeveless, button down shirt, the kind I can't resist buying even now when I stumble upon one in a consignment store. Her hair is dark, short. I am wearing a white dress, white socks, patent leather shoes. My mother, the town girl, bringing her farm baby for a ride on the corn chopper. My hair is also dark. No curls yet. My hand is opened across my mother's shoulder. The knob of my mother's shoulder. She will no doubt be wondering how it is I love my father as much as I do. She will already be thinking this. Did she love him then? Love him still? Is it love that made her carry his baby out to him, to stand in a place she never imagined standing? I'm sure I did ride that day, the chopper idling as my father swung down and lifted me from my mother's arms. He would have gotten my dress dirty. I would not have wanted to leave him. I remember those fields for all the harvests after that one, the dry stalks' susurrations, the gopher holes along the now exposed stone walls, the world with both my parents in it.

Despite Everything

It was the summer an eagle flew over Steve's house
just as we stood outside to say goodbye, the summer
sleek, oily bear cubs rolled through mulch at Jon's.
Four deer grazed in the field, and a turkey pair
bookended their brood in a neighbor's driveway.
The groundhog had groundhogs and they nibbled
clover, tunneled into the garden. Coyotes
big as wolves attacked a dog. Outside the gate,
a garter snake lunged at guests, but the feral cat
let us draw close enough to see his broken teeth.
Hummingbirds on the Rose of Sharon. The same
fat toad on the walkway. We took nothing as a sign.
Not the white sharks off the coast. Not the hornets'
nest that clogged the screech owl house. The apple
trees finally blossomed. Everything was hungry
or sated, hunting or fat, pink mouthed, sugared—
a small world balanced out the corner of our eye.

My mother would have thought I am crazy for bringing this up, but

this pigeon's eyes are closed.
It's hard to imagine a pigeon might die in its sleep.
I hadn't considered that pigeons die at all.

There are so many pigeons. Shouldn't we see more dead ones?
(And shouldn't we, confronted with any evidence,
have questions more profound?)

And now: to step over it or to move it from this path?
With a shovel if that were easy to procure.
With a discarded pizza box.

No one likes to consider matters of disposal.
No one likes to think about purgatory, either, though when I imagine it,
I think of a sink drain, the bits of onion skin, the lone noodle it collects.

I wonder what swoops in to remove dead pigeons? If something
waits for me to step away? Wonder what happens
if no place exists in which to work towards forgiveness?

The Girl I Wronged Grew Up to Be a Healer

I saw her once, after many years,
in front of me at a yield sign.

I thought she'd gone
and edged forward, tapped her bumper.

(I should have gotten out of the car
to apologize, at least for the obvious.

To have finally gotten it over with.

Should have said, *It won't matter,*
but I got what was coming to me.

Spent my life teaching the great tragedies,
the filthy contrails of hubris.

Lessons part admonition, part regret.

I might have cautioned my students:
Even forgiveness will not alter who you were.)

We had hated how happy this girl
insisted on being.

How she burst into our world
in braids that reminded us of goat huts, chalets.

Her speed on the playground.

How happy she was to see us,
to open her math book, to be up at bat.

Happy at lunch, leaving lunch.
Happy to line up once recess ended.

Happy walking to school in the rain,
loaning a pencil, passing a tissue, waiting her turn.

Insistent, persistent, unwavering joy.

We wanted nothing to do with her happiness
and she could not see fit to distance herself from it.

It was as simple an equation as that.

These were the days of pace-yourself, open-loft mathematics.
This was the only kind of computation we mastered.

Our teacher was happy in her student's happiness.
Otherwise, our teacher was never happy.

She reeked of powder, layers of the kind of skin
that bruises as easily as a ripe peach
in the bottom of the bag.

But there was nothing to this girl's kind of happiness.

So we wrote notes and stuffed her desk with them,
brainstormed nasty names for her.
Pointed out what she'd been blind to.

She told the teacher. The teacher told the principal
who called us to his office.

We thought we were getting an award.
We'd made brotherhood posters that week,
 planted trees along the bus drop off area.

Separated by kids we'd never choose to sit by,
we wrote apologies we didn't mean, gave up
the one friend who decided to like her.

Even now, she smiles. Waves as she drives off
to open her hand over the afflicted,
to divine heat and vibrations.

I hope she didn't recognize me. That she never
has to come across my name.

Girl, I should have written, no matter that
I was nine years old. *I will always be sorry for this.*

She could have taught me about the space
that must be reserved for pain.

Mirrorless as I had been.

If You Normally Turn Right Out of Your Driveway, Turn Left, Instead

To spark neural pathways dulled by routine, I head uphill and, instantly

    I want—

the Victorian on the corner, its three sheep, its double-cordoned grapevines.

    The long driveway to a house on a hill with the view

        of Ipswich Bay.

The artist's studio. A power washer and a pickup truck to use it on.

    The birdhouse vacant of purple martins and to be

           a purple martin who is somewhere
      else and to be

    the house's waiting "o", and the return flight, the reunion of mosquito eaters.

Is this how it works?

    The singed and snapping runnels leading solely to envy?

I want to be both horses, separate paddocks, who roll

        onto their backs to rub their blankets off—

to be them and their blankets and their purpose

and the ones who ignore them
and keep grazing.

I want the gelding's chestnut hindquarters and especially, most

painfully, the Paint mare's white,

quite

glamorous

tail.

Dear Cousin Who Declares Me Matriarch

You didn't come for the funeral. Instead, you wrote: *You must be the big mama now*. Matriarch, I heard. Elephants. Famiglia. The Madonna in our nonnie's peonies. Remember when you were relieved I wasn't a lesbian: *We were worried about you. We thought, you know, you might be a little funny*. We. A pronoun that kept me up at night wondering who, which ones? Our aunts in the kind of lawn chairs that required rewebbing, our uncles tossing horseshoes, pausing mid-throw to listen. Now, you need help making peace with your brother. My brother left the country with our mother's colander, her sharpest knife. My mother loved knives. *I do regret*, she finally admitted, *stabbing Sam and slashing Herbie's tires. I shouldn't have done those things*. But Sam touched her when she told him not to. Herbie was having an affair. They were—you are—all knives, and, yet, she wielded you. I'm no matriarch. No sword swallower. You slice something open, you live with it. Praise its scarry imperfection. I cut my thieving brother off. Your brother did the same. And, Cousin, I do love women. Especially those who might have healed us, proclaimed the suture a kind of peace. Those women never needed men. But in this you are correct: They're gone.

The Spoon

From the second house we've emptied
this year, my husband sorts metal into piles—
gutter elbows, drill bits, copper pipe.
All our parents are dead now.
I have learned what I do not want
to know: This hot summer is not
aberration. It is precursor.
I sit before the fan, barricade myself
with laundry baskets so the dog
can't get too close, cover my feet
with her unthinkable fur. My husband
puts a tarnished spoon on the table.
Silver, he says. As if this will lift
a curtain like a breeze. As if, suddenly,
we will walk barefoot through frost.
But this spoon is another item of which
we must now dispose. This legacy
of stuff that is as stultifying as August.
Cardboard shirt boxes, belleek china,
electrical cords taped with electrical tape,
body bags of t-shirts and socks. But not,
no never again, my mother bending
over a word search, or leaving talc
footprints across the carpet after her bath.
What does my husband imagine I will do
with this spoon? How can it possibly
matter? *If you were a precious metal,*
mined from the earth's crust, is this
what you would choose to be? I ask
the spoon. The mute spoon. This spoon

with its history of polishing, tarnishing,
of lips and tongues. This spoon which reflects
no light, registers neither desire nor regret,
what is coming, what is already gone.

What They Might Have Missed About Him
When He Went Off to War

The way he stirred his coffee too long.
The way he mulled things—what might fix
a busted auger, cure a calf of scours.

The way rote tasks—harrowing
the last field, supper ignored—quieted his head.
A blackened thumbnail.

There are times I forget that he loved laurel,
lady slippers, Bob Whites. Times when I lay in bed
listening for his spoon to stop.

Some things he would not rush: Milkings.
Mornings. Prying splinters
from my palm with a jackknife blade.

They say he caught pneumonia
hauling seaweed one December.
They say his asthma came from that.

So, there was his coughing. How it started
sometimes when he tried to answer
a question, sing a Dean Martin song.

His webby windpipe. The terrible lungs.
Also the membranous skin patched onto his legs.
How easily it bled.

Though that would have been later.
After the war.
His sleeplessness and lack of appetite.

It was all the sugar he used, that stirring.
It was ritual. They say he used to pray. They say
the cows gave less milk when he was gone.

Mourning my mother, I almost forget

the last phone call with my father who told me he was excited
for dinner. Baked shrimp, buttery breadcrumbs.
They feed you pretty good there, I said. *How's the fever?*

The fever persisted and no one all those hours away
seemed concerned. He was looking forward to a hospital meal.
A man who never had an appetite.

He would have waited, hands folded atop the bedsheet,
at the end of a life with so little stillness,
for the tray that might arrive any moment.

Instead, the tumor burst through the wall of his colon.
He should have been in enormous pain, the doctors said.
The doctors who had missed a tumor the size of a football

in a man who weighed one hundred thirty-five pounds.
The human body is full of organs, someone said.
Some useless sage. *Things aren't as easy to find as you might think.*

As I might think, no. A high school teacher. A poet. You could
swallow
a Volkswagen Beetle and I might not be able to distinguish it
from gall bladder or lung. But a doctor?

Aren't those the people who hid their lab notes from me
in chemistry class so, god forbid, I wouldn't cheat?
Is this what they prevented? My pursuit of their blessed science?

It isn't fair either how much my mother's death has made him
less. It isn't his fault he went first,
that it has been months since I've pictured him

in his bed alone, waiting for his shrimp. Imagined me
in my terrible apartment standing one second longer
over the telephone, I, who had always feared his death.

Those last years, he called me Wednesday nights. My mother
out playing cards. The barns empty. The fields overgrown.
I loved picturing him in from the cold.

The Stationary Lungs of Hawks

Red-tails love open fields, alfalfa flashing goldfinch. Love clouds at their backs, the spoon-silver water of ponds, hills mooning up green and full of prey. Their lungs fill holes in bones. Some of this I know. Some I have inferred.

My father, an asthmatic, tried to teach me: pay attention. But we earthly beings, we drivers and walkers, pass the field at the end of our street each morning and feel solely purposeful. We see no explosions of gold, no rufous tail, aloft and circling, that should be so impossible to miss.

The red-tail mating dance is high altitude, an aerial display. And when, finally, he latches on, they tuck their wings and freefall.

Our own bodies do not allow this kind of love. We weigh ourselves down with exhalations. Our lungs do too much work.

Notes

"Smart Girls Always Have a Plan" page 23: "Math is movement trying to express itself" is from Claire Voisin (b 1962); French Professor of Mathematics; director of research at the Institut de mathématiques de Jussieu at the University of Paris VI: Pierre et Marie Curie.

"The Mere Pleasure of God" page 43: Title and some textual references from "Sinners in the Hands of an Angry God" by Jonathan Edwards, 1741.

Acknowledgements

The author would like to thank the editors of the following journals in which these poems or earlier versions of these poems have appeared.

Carolina Quarterly Review: "In the Movie of my Dreams of You" and "Phantom"
Comstock Review: "As If Faith Has Anything To Do With It"
Connecticut Poetry Review: "The Spoon"
descant: "My Mother Would Have Thought I Am Crazy for Bringing This Up, But" (as "Considerations")
Empty House: "Wishful" (as "You Would Have Loved It There")
Euphony: "Parable" (as "Memoir")
Iron Horse Literary Review: "Offertorium"
Italian Americana: "Reliquary, Shadowbox" (as "The Time of Year to Consider Lamplighters"), "This Nothing Like Forgiveness", and "Despite Everything"
Los Angeles Review: "Feast"
Lily Poetry Review: "For Homework I Told Sixteen Girls to Break Some Rules" (as "For Homework I Told Three Girls to Break Some Rules")
Mom Egg Review: "To the Specialist", "Our Boldest Child", "Heirloom", "Like Enough, Like Belonging" (as "From Has Never Happened to This"); "Winter Baby"
Ovunque Siamo: "Sunday Nights the Widows Came to Dinner", "What They Might Have Missed About Him When He Went off to War", "Dear Cousin Who Declares Me Matriarch", and "Mourning my mother, I almost forget"
Pithead Chapel: "The Stationary Lungs of Hawks", "The Riparian Dreams of Hawks", "The Requirements of an Injured Hawk"
Poetry: "Someone Asks Me to Consider Time"
Ponder Review: "After My Mother Requests a Parent-Teacher Conference"

Reed Magazine: "From the Hollow Ends of Pipe, Yellow Jackets Stung Our Lips When We Tried to Trumpet" (as "Swingset, 1968")
Riverteeth: "In the Car She Drives, the Air is Always Fresh(ened)"
San Pedro River Review: "The Mere Pleasure of God"
Saranac Review: "Innocence", and "Orchid Hour"
Spillway: "Midwife in the Cowbarn"
Two Hawks Quarterly: "When We Come Without Our Daughters and Still Leave Them Behind" and "On Days Like This"
Unbroken: "Artifact, September 1963"
Water-Stone Review: "Smart Girls Always Have a Plan"

For many years, my high school students and I set up a poetry stand all over the North Shore of Massachusetts. The kids wrote hundreds of poems on the spot for customers who ordered them. We never charged, never accepted tips. Our goal was to spread poetry. As a writer who eventually decided to teach, I prided myself on being able to say that I hadn't asked my students to do anything with their own writing that I hadn't done, but I had never written poems by request—until I began work on some of the poems that would become this manuscript. Then, I reached out to people (though not strangers) and invited them to order poems. I am grateful for the ways in which their requests forced me to grow as a poet, to examine topics I would otherwise never have considered. My thanks to all those who responded, whether or not their poems appear in this book. I dedicate the poems below as follows:

Feast for Melissa Aureli

For Homework, I Told Sixteen Girls to Break Some Rules for Olivia Anderson, Joy Bergner, Moira Callahan, Gabby D'Agostino, Emily DeMarco, Cami Devoe, Cammie Foley, Caroline Foley, Michaela Hedderman, Lilly Kallman, Olivia Kubaska, Isabella Liderbach, Laura McCormack, Alison Nunziato, Ciara O'Flynn Gillis, and Amelia Young.

From the Hollow Ends of Pipe, Yellow Jackets Stung Our Lips When We Tried to Trumpet for Linda Buddenhagen

In the Movie of my Dreams of You for Teresa Starkey

Phantom for Holly Robinson

Reliquary, Shadowbox for Jo Pendola

Smart Girls Always Have a Plan for Colleen Cavanagh

Someone Asks Me to Consider Time for Sharon Fish

What There Was to Fall From for Cathy Lange

What They Might Have Missed About Him When He Went Off to War for Linda Panciera

Why I Don't Keep a Diary for Anna Gibbs

Other dedications:

Wishful for Cindy Veach

If You Normally Turn Left Out of Your Driveway, Turn Right Instead for Penny Hurley

The Requirements of an Injured Hawk for Rebecca Kinzie Bastian

Parable for Louis Cimalore Jr

I'm honored to work again with Bordighera Press and am grateful to Fred Gardaphé, Paolo Giordano, and Anthony Julian Tamburri and to Nicholas Grosso for all of his help with this manuscript. I am thankful, too, for support of the Italian American Writers Association.

I'm also grateful for a community of poets whose work has inspired me and whose insight strengthened these poems: Kevin Carey, M.P Carver, Eileen Cleary, Lis Horowitz, Jennifer Jean, Dawn Jones, Kirun

Kapur, Julia Lisella, January O'Neill, Dawn Paul, Lynn Potts, and J.D. Scrimgeour.

And for the Salem Writers Group, and for Poetry Cleanse poets and Cleanse coordinators Jeanne Obbard and Jane Hart.

Also for the more than 200 Ipswich High School student poets who fearlessly staffed the Poetry Stand, and to our customers who trusted us with their ideas.

Special love and thanks to Scott Withiam, and to fellow Good Harbor poets: K.T. Landon, Kali Lightfoot, Jennifer Martelli, Cindy Veach and Rebecca Olander (with extra love for coming up with the book's title).

Belated thanks to Joe Antonio for telling me, all those years ago: "Take a poetry class. You'll love it." Also a belated apology for thinking he was out of his mind.

Rebecca Kinzie Bastian, you are both midwife and doula of this book and so many of its poems. So much love and thanks for all your gifts, especially that of your friendship.

Thanks always to my parents, Aldo and Mary Panciera who nurtured dreams very different than their own.

To Dennis, and to our daughters, Beatrice, Apphia, and Justina, thank you for all that is best about my life. Can't say enough how much I love you.

About the Author

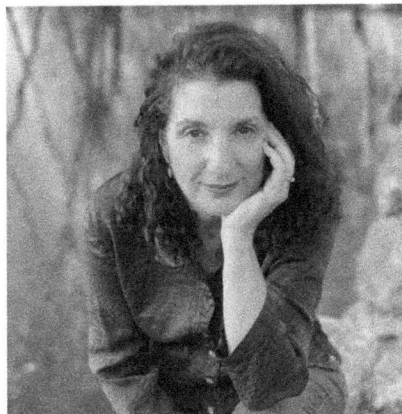

CARLA PANCIERA was raised on her family's dairy farm in Westerly, RI.

She has published two previous collections of poetry: Cider Press Award Winner, *One of the Cimalores* and Bordighera Press Poetry Award Winning, *No Day, No Dusk, No Love*. Her poetry has appeared in numerous magazines including *Poetry, RHINO, Cream City Review,* and the *Los Angeles Review*.

Her collection of short stories, *Bewildered*, received the 2013 Grace Paley Short Fiction Award from the Association of Writers and Writing Programs and was published by the University of Massachusetts Press.

Her short stories have appeared in the *New England Review*, the *Clackamas Review, Slice,* and other magazines. Her short story, "The Kind of People Who Look at Art" was indexed as a distinguished story in Best American Short Stories 2017 by Junot Diaz.

She was the James E. Kilgore scholar in Nonfiction at Bread Loaf Writers Conference and is the recipient of an Individual Artist Grant in Creative Nonfiction from the Massachusetts Cultural Council. She is also the author *Barnflower: A Rhode Island Farm Memoir* (Loom Press, 2023).

A recently retired high school English teacher, Carla lives on the North Shore of Massachusetts.

LUIGI RUSTICHELLI, Ed. *Seminario sul racconto*. Vol 16. Narrative.

LEWIS TURCO. *Shaking the Family Tree*. Vol 15. Memoirs.

LUIGI RUSTICHELLI, Ed. *Seminario sulla drammaturgia*.
Vol 14. Theater/Essays.

FRED GARDAPHÈ. *Moustache Pete is Dead! Long Live Moustache Pete!*.
Vol 13. Oral Literature.

JONE GAILLARD CORSI. *Il libretto d'autore. 1860 - 1930*. Vol 12. Criticism.

HELEN BAROLINI. *Chiaroscuro: Essays of Identity*. Vol 11. Essays.

PICARAZZI & FEINSTEIN, Eds. *An African Harlequin in Milan*.
Vol 10. Theater/Essays.

JOSEPH RICAPITO. *Florentine Streets & Other Poems*. Vol 9. Poetry.

FRED MISURELLA. *Short Time*. Vol 8. Novella.

NED CONDINI. *Quartettsatz*. Vol 7. Poetry.

ANTHONY JULIAN TAMBURRI, Ed. *Fuori: Essays by Italian/American Lesbiansand Gays*. Vol 6. Essays.

ANTONIO GRAMSCI. P. Verdicchio. Trans. & Intro. *The Southern Question*.
Vol 5. Social Criticism.

DANIELA GIOSEFFI. *Word Wounds & Water Flowers*. Vol 4. Poetry. $8

WILEY FEINSTEIN. *Humility's Deceit: Calvino Reading Ariosto Reading Calvino*.
Vol 3. Criticism.

PAOLO A. GIORDANO, Ed. *Joseph Tusiani: Poet. Translator. Humanist*.
Vol 2. Criticism.

ROBERT VISCUSI. *Oration Upon the Most Recent Death of Christopher Columbus*.
Vol 1. Poetry.

www.ingramcontent.com/pod-product-compliance
Lightning Source LLC
Chambersburg PA
CBHW020210090426
42734CB00008B/1010